On Monday, I went to the zoo.
Guess who followed me home?

A gorilla!
I asked my mom if he could stay.
"If he is a good guest," Mom said.

On Tuesday, Gorilla broke Granny's glasses and gabbed on the phone all day.

On Wednesday, Gorilla trampled the grapes growing in the garden.

On Thursday, Gorilla gobbled up
a gooseberry pie, a gallon of ice cream,
and other goodies.

On Friday, Gorilla dressed like a ghost
and scared the goldfish.

On Saturday, Gorilla glued gumdrops
to Dad's galoshes.

On Sunday, Gorilla invited a gang of friends over.
The gorillas played golf and other games.

They made a great mess.

"That gorilla must go!" Mom said.

"He has been a terrible guest!"

On Monday, I went to visit Gorilla at the zoo.
Guess who followed me home?

How many things can you find that begin with the letter G?

Gg Cheer

G is for gorillas, on the loose

G is for gopher, goldfish, and goose

G is for granny, giggle, and glass

G is for gumdrops, grapes, and grass

Hooray for **G**, big and small—

the grandest, greatest letter of all!